The Book Corner

Written by Sarah Russell
Illustrated by Caroline Keys

"Why are you sad, Lily?" asked Mr Earle.

"I miss Book Corner," said Lily.

Mr Earle nodded his head. "Harry misses it, too," he said. "But there is no room for it in this classroom."

"There is," said Harry. "Lily and I will draw a plan to show where it can go."

Mr Earle nodded again.

Lily got paper and Harry got pencils. "We will show you, Mr Earle!" they said.

Harry and Lily sat at their table. They talked about the plan.

"We don't need two play areas," said Harry.

"No we don't," said Lily. "And that bookshelf can stay there."

"Yes," said Harry.

“What are you doing?” asked Ari.

“We are drawing a plan,” said Lily. “It will show where a new Book Corner can go.”

“I can help you build it,” said Ari.

Harry and Lily drew a plan. Mr Earle helped them write the words.

The plan showed where the new Book Corner could go.

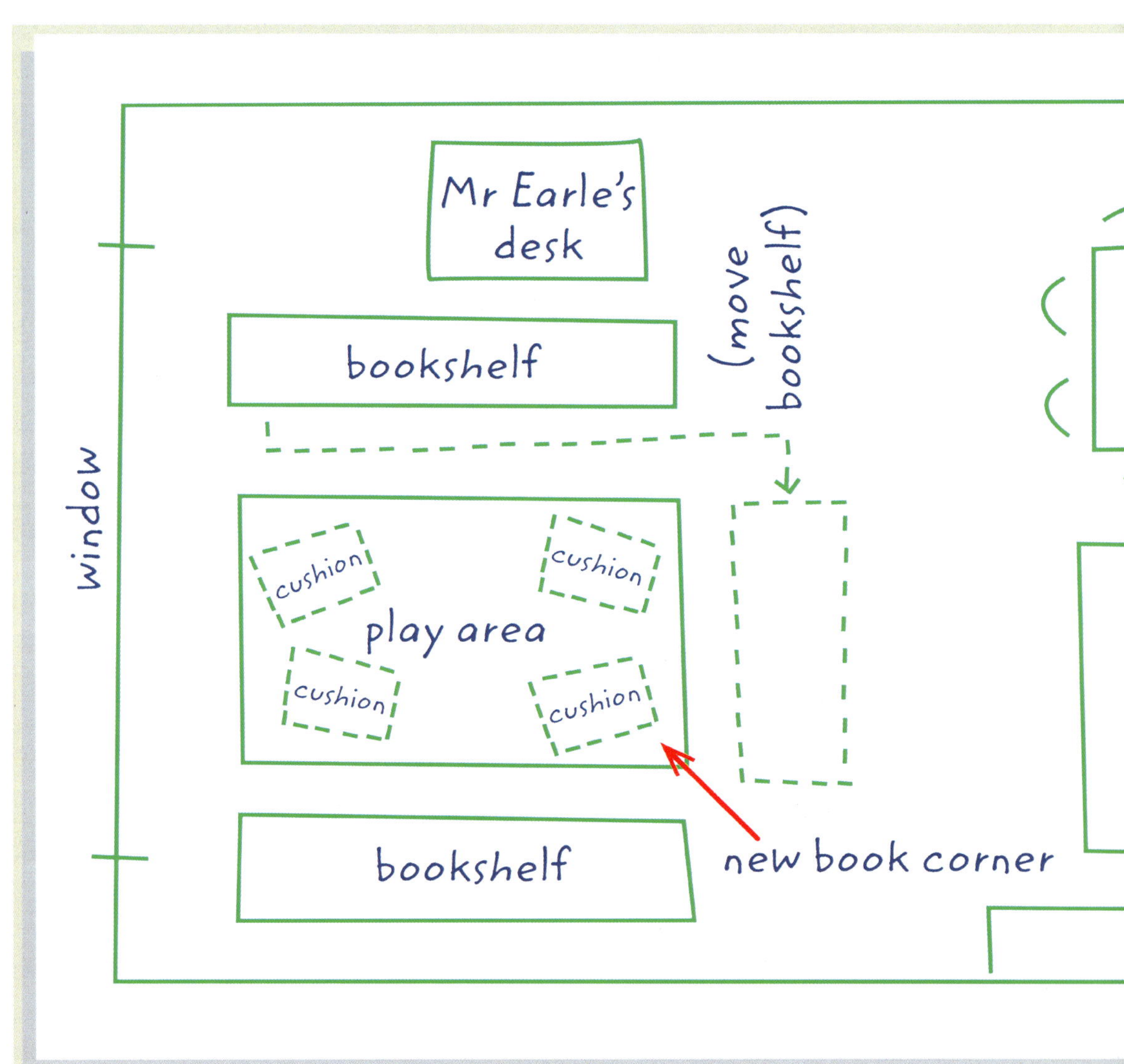

There was one bookshelf to move. The toys in the old play area needed to move, too. They could go in the other play area near the door.

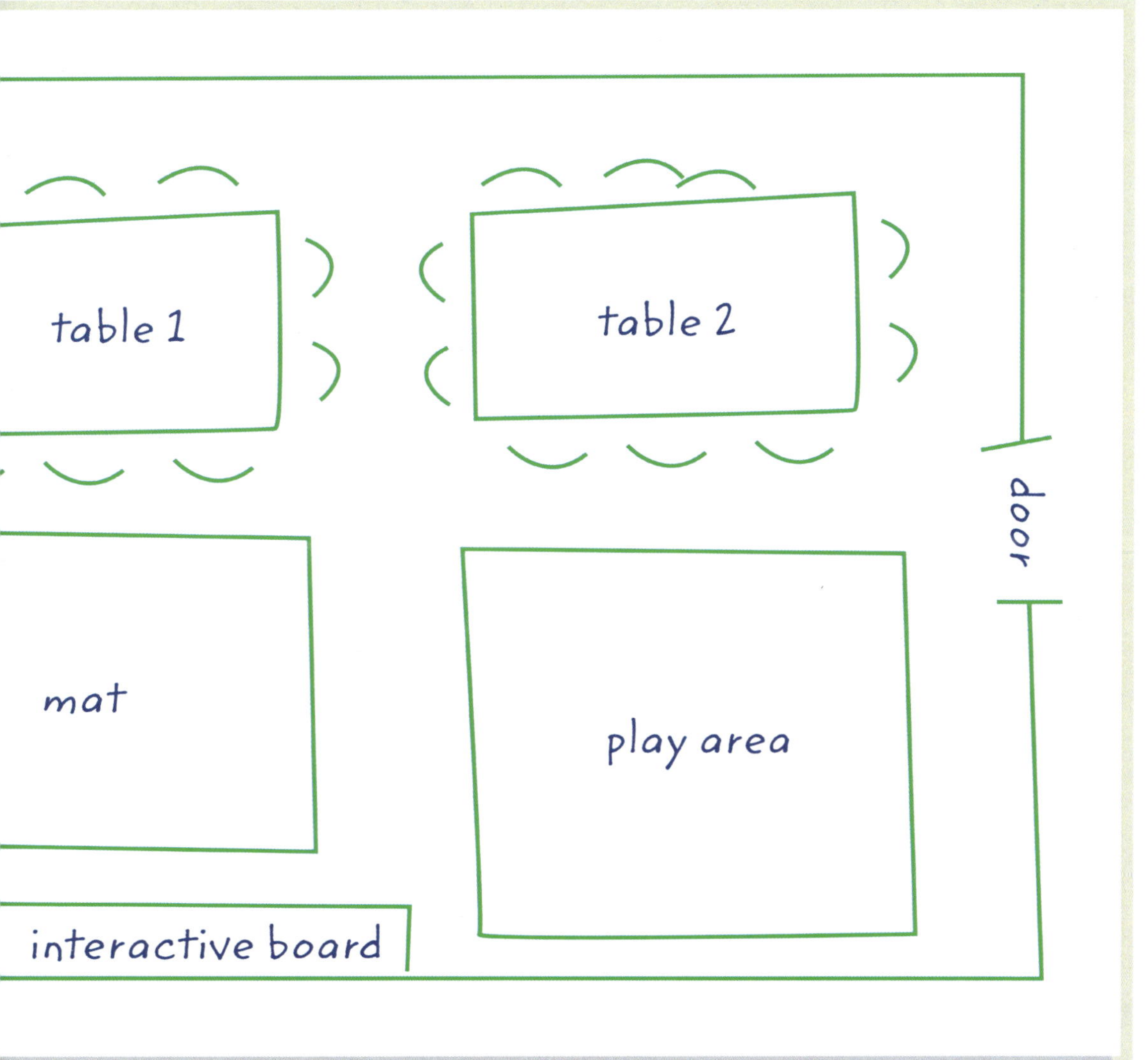

Lily and Harry showed Mr Earle their plan.

"It is a good plan," he said. "You can show it to the class."

All the children sat on the floor.

"Lily and Harry want to show you their plan," said Mr Earle. "It shows where we can have a new Book Corner."

Lily and Harry showed their plan.

"It looks great!" said the children.

The next day, Ari helped Harry and Lily move all the toys. Then they took the books off the bookshelf and Mr Earle moved it.

Ari and Lily put all the books back into the bookshelf. Harry got cushions from the store room. He put them on the floor of the new Book Corner.

"The new Book Corner is ready to use!" said Lily and Harry.

"Well done, Lily, Harry and Ari," said Mr Earle. "It is great!"